Science
and
Sustainable
Construction

Carla Mooney

San Diego, CA

© 2018 ReferencePoint Press, Inc.
Printed in the United States

For more information, contact:
ReferencePoint Press, Inc.
PO Box 27779
San Diego, CA 92198
www.ReferencePointPress.com

LIBRARY OF CONGRESS CATALOGING-IN-PUBLICATION DATA

Name: Mooney, Carla, 1970– author.
Title: Science and Sustainable Construction/by Carla Mooney.
Description: San Diego, CA: ReferencePoint Press, Inc., 2018. | Series: Science and Sustainability | Includes bibliographical references and index.
Identifiers: LCCN 2017016047 (print) | LCCN 2017023059 (ebook) | ISBN 9781682822562 (eBook) | ISBN 9781682822555 (hardback)
Subjects: LCSH: Sustainable construction.
Classification: LCC TH880 (ebook) | LCC TH880 .M665 2018 (print) | DDC 690.028/6--dc23
LC record available at https://lccn.loc.gov/2017016047

CONTENTS

INTRODUCTION

Building a
Sustainable World

Around the world, sustainability is a hot topic, even though many people do not know exactly what it means. For some people, the concept of sustainability is synonymous with protecting the environment. However, sustainability involves much more than being environmentally friendly.

Achieving sustainability means considering and balancing the needs of the environment, economy, and society. When it comes to the environment, sustainable practices ensure that humans consume earth's natural resources in a way that does not damage the environment and ecosystems and does not deplete natural resources too quickly. A holistic view of sustainability also considers the economy and a region's need for current and future jobs, for economic growth, and for businesses to use resources efficiently and responsibly for the long term. Finally, when thinking about sustainability, humans must consider the needs of society, particularly the well-being of people living in each community, each country, and the world. It involves providing equal opportunities for all people, reducing poverty, and preserving peace. These three pillars of sustainability—environment, economy, and society—are interconnected and depend on each other. Steve Walker, manager of environmental sustainability at Burt's Bees, says:

> I like to say that environmental and social sustainability are enabled by financial sustainability. You can't work in the former spaces if you're not tending to the latter as well. However, organizations have a responsibility to consider not only how they may minimize their environmental footprint but, ultimately, [how they may] have a net positive impact on the environment as a whole.[1]

What Is Sustainable Construction?

In the construction industry, buildings and other structures can have a significant impact on earth's sustainable future. According to the Organisation for Economic Co-operation and Development, buildings in developed countries account for more than 40 percent of energy consumption over their lifetime—through raw material production, construction, operation, maintenance, and decommissioning (the shutdown or removal of a building). With more than half of the world's population living in urban environments, construction has a significant role in earth's sustainable future. The need to develop sustainable buildings is more urgent today than ever.

Sustainable construction means working to meet human needs for housing, places to work, and other infrastructure without negatively affecting the ability of future people to meet their own needs. Sustainable practices consider a building project's long-term impact on the environment, community, and economy. Sustainable buildings efficiently use energy, water, and other resources. They are built with safe materials to help protect the health of occupants, and are designed to improve employee productivity. They also reduce waste, pollution, and environmental

The residential towers known as Bosco Verticale (Vertical Forest) in Milan, Italy, feature more than nine hundred trees on the terraces of the two buildings. The trees help reduce smog and produce oxygen. They also moderate building temperatures and soften noise.

damage. "Sustainable development must be an integrated agenda for economic, environmental, and social solutions," writes Ban Ki-moon, United Nations secretary-general. "Responding to all goals as a cohesive and integrated whole will be critical to ensuring the transformations needed at scale."[2]

Science and Sustainable Construction

Around the world, sustainability experts are looking for innovative ways to build and maintain cities. Green construction projects incorporate recycled materials, green roofs for rainwater management, natural ventilation systems, and other innovations. Zero-energy buildings generate as much renewable energy as they use. Engineers and architects are designing sustainable urban drainage systems and low-irrigation landscaping called xeriscaping, as well as testing renewable energy sources.

Sustainable construction is gaining popularity around the world. According to the World Green Building Trends 2016 report by Dodge Data & Analytics, more than 60 percent of building projects for those surveyed would be sustainable by 2018. The report gathered information about sustainable construction from more than one thousand architects, engineers, contractors, owners, specialists, and consultants in sixty-nine countries. The largest percentage of sustainable building activity was in the commercial building segment, with growth also projected for institutional buildings such as schools, hospitals, and other public buildings. According to the report, the demand for sustainable construction is being driven by both client demand for sustainable projects (40 percent) and environmental regulations (35 percent). A greater awareness of the benefits of sustainable construction for building occupants and neighborhoods was also noted as a driver of sustainable construction demand. "Green building activity continues to accelerate, with growing awareness of occupant and tenant benefits, speaking to the fact that the real, tangible benefits of green buildings are becoming more widely recognized,"[3] says John Mandyck, chief sustainability officer at United Technologies Corporation.

Science and technology are a key part of these innovations. Scientists are developing new technologies and designing new processes to support sustainable construction. These innovations range from renewable energy and water reuse systems to air-quality improvement and building components made from recycled materials.

From Textile Waste to Sustainable Panels

In 2016 researchers from the Technical University of Madrid in Spain announced they had developed a way to use textile waste to create a sustainable wall panel that could be used in construction. Textile waste is discarded clothing, along with fabric, remnants, and scraps from the textile manufacturing process. In the European Union approximately 6.4 million tons (5.8 million metric tons) of textile waste is discarded annually. Only about 25 percent of the waste is recycled, with 4.7 million tons (4.3 million metric tons) being incinerated or stored in landfills. The university researchers used some of this textile waste to produce interior panels, which could be used to create inner partitions and walls in new construction and building renovations. Because the textile waste was remnants from manufacturing offcuts or threads and already met quality standards for human use, it did not need any special treatment in order to be safe.

> **WORDS IN CONTEXT**
>
> **xeriscaping**
>
> Landscaping in a way that needs little to no irrigation.

The university researchers developed a binder textile fiber by blending the waste with natural hydraulic lime, which has excellent properties to safeguard against fires and contaminant emissions. Not only does the recycled panel provide a use for textile waste, it has several advantages over other panels on the market. A textile fiber panel has a lower density than other panels, which lightens the load on the panel's support systems. In addition, the panel has better thermal and sound absorption than other panels on the market because of the use of textile fibers.

By using recycled materials, the manufacturing process for the panels uses significantly less energy than does the production of new construction materials. Also, using recycled materials reduces the need for incineration of waste or storage at landfills, both of which impact the environment unfavorably through the release of greenhouse gas emissions.

Science and Technology for a Sustainable Future

Science and technology will play a critical role in the future of sustainability and sustainable construction. Through science, communities will be able to build structures that meet the needs of the environment, economy, and society. At the present, says Ban Ki-moon, "we live in a period of unprecedented technological innovation and change. New technologies are unlocking possibilities for sustainable development. The solutions that they can generate, and the levels of access that they can enable, will be crucial to our vision for the world."[4]

CHAPTER ONE

History of Sustainable Construction

> **"Experiencing the need for change is the first step towards mainstreaming sustainability."**

—Sally Uren, chief executive officer of Forum for the Future

Sally Uren, "How to Help Someone Experience the Need for Change," *Green Futures*, October 2013, p. 35. https://issuu.com.

Although sustainable construction has been a popular idea in recent years, sustainable building techniques have been used in buildings and structures for many years. For example, London's Crystal Palace used construction methods that minimized the building's impact on the environment. Built in 1851 for the Great Exhibition in London's Hyde Park, the Crystal Palace was a huge glass and iron structure. Because sunlight shone through its clear glass walls and ceilings, the palace did not need interior lights. Architects designed the building's roof using a minimum amount of materials. They were also able to maintain a comfortable temperature in the glass building by using underground air-cooling chambers that drew cooler air through small gaps in the flooring while also allowing hot air to escape through louvres in the building's outer walls.

Sustainable building practices such as those used in the Crystal Palace increased the efficiency with which buildings used energy, water, and materials and also reduced their impact on human health and the environment. These early designs and practices would lead the way for further development and innovation in sustainable building.

Late Nineteenth and Early Twentieth Centuries

In the early twentieth century, electrical heating and cooling were not common in buildings. To control interior temperatures, architects used a combination of mechanical devices and passive techniques to ventilate high-rise and long buildings. Mechanical steam systems heated many large buildings; however, they often had trouble effectively distributing the steam heat and condensation. To supplement these systems, passive design techniques were used to keep buildings cool, such as setting windows deep into the facade of a building to shield them from the heat of the sun. Built in 1904, the New York Times Building featured deep-set windows at the top to shield the most exposed part of the building from the sun and control interior temperatures. In New York's Flatiron Building, built in 1902, designers set windows deep into the thermally absorbing stone facade to reduce heat from the sun. In Chicago retractable awnings over the Carson Pirie Scott department store's windows blocked the sun's rays from entering the windows, helping keep interior temperatures cool during hot summer months. When building occupants wanted to cool temperatures in the building, they could extend the awnings to block the sun. When they wanted to use the sun to heat the building, they could raise the awnings to let the sunlight in the windows. Other commercial buildings of the era used window shades to help control the sun's exposure.

> **WORDS IN CONTEXT**
>
> **passive design**
> A type of design that takes advantage of the climate to maintain comfortable indoor temperatures in order to reduce or eliminate the use of mechanical systems.

In many early buildings, air-extraction systems were built into the floors and ceilings of structures to help ventilate the buildings. Long buildings such as train stations and exhibition halls often had ventilation systems built into the peaks of the roof. These systems worked on the principle that hot air rises and creates an updraft. Vents in the roof allowed hot air and moisture to escape from the building as the air rose, while the updraft pulled in cooler

London's Crystal Palace, built in 1851 for the Great Exhibition, was designed to have minimal impact on the environment. The huge glass and iron structure (pictured) relied on sunlight rather than interior lighting and a system of underground cooling chambers for temperature control.

air through ground-level vents. In 1877 Giuseppe Mengoni, the designer of the Galleria Vittorio Emanuele II in Milan, Italy, created a new solution to ventilate a long-span building. He designed a system called a labyrinth that pulled inside air into underground chambers, where it was cooled by the earth and then returned to the building through floor vents.

New Technologies Transform Construction

Beginning in the 1930s several new building technologies transformed urban construction. The invention of air-conditioning, fluorescent lighting, reflective glass, and structural steel made it possible to build enormous skyscrapers and long-span mall structures. Because fossil fuels were cheap and readily available, massive heating, ventilation, and air-conditioning (HVAC) systems powered by these fuels heated and cooled the buildings. Architects were more focused on incorporating air-conditioning into their tall buildings than thinking about the impact these systems might have on the environment.

Buildings made of glass and steel rose, without operating windows, ventilators, awnings, or window shades. Because fluorescent lighting did not emit much heat, architects could widen the floor plan of buildings and create spaces that could be comfortably lit with only artificial lighting. Interior spaces no longer needed to be near windows for natural light.

After World War II the United States experienced an economic boom, which led to an explosion in building projects. Popular glass and steel box-style buildings littered the landscape of the country's urban and suburban communities. These buildings consumed massive amounts of energy to heat, cool, and illuminate, which made them dependent on the availability of low-cost fossil fuel energy sources.

Rising Fuel Costs Spur Changes

In the 1970s a small group of architects and environmentalists began to question the impact building structures had on communities and the environment. They urged builders to rethink the energy used in buildings and the materials used in construction. Then in 1973 an oil crisis brought fossil fuels to the attention of the American public. The Yom Kippur War, a war between a coalition of Arab states and Israel, broke out in early October. The decision of Western countries to send aid to Israel angered several Arab nations, which were some of the largest oil producers in the world. In response, the Organization of the Petroleum Exporting Countries decided to significantly cut oil production. This action triggered a shortage of fuel in the United States and other countries around the world. Gasoline prices skyrocketed and gas station lines stretched for blocks. The cost of heating and cooling buildings rose significantly, as did production costs for construction materials that used fossil fuels.

Many Americans began to wonder how to reduce the country's reliance on fossil fuels. To help address this problem, the American Institute of Architects created an energy task force. Part of the group investigated passive systems that could be used to reduce energy use, such as reflective roofing materials and environmentally friendly sites for buildings. Another part of the task force researched technological solutions such as triple-glazed windows, which help keep heat from escaping a building. US and Western European government researchers also focused on reducing energy consumption in commercial and single-family buildings.

Green Building Gains Momentum

In this energy-conscious environment, the green building movement gained momentum in the 1970s. Efforts to create buildings that conserved energy increased. In the United States, California commissioned eight energy-efficient state office buildings. One of the most famous, the Gregory Bateson Building, built in 1978 in Sacramento, used passive heating and cooling systems. For example, rocks were placed under the first floor to help retain cool air that came from the earth. The cool air was then released into office spaces. The builders also installed energy-generating equipment such as photovoltaic systems, which converted sunlight into electricity.

In England, where fossil fuel prices were even higher than in the United States, architects strived to incorporate natural lighting, ventilation, and renewable power sources in buildings. They used ideas from older buildings that had incorporated passive techniques, as well new technologies such as generating energy through solar cells and wind turbines. One example of a green building was the Willis Faber & Dumas Headquarters, built in Ipswich between 1970 and 1975. The building's walls were made from glass panels that were mirrored to reduce heat gain and allow

> **WORDS IN CONTEXT**
>
> **photovoltaics**
>
> The conversion of light into electricity using semiconducting materials.

14

The Willis Faber & Dumas Headquarters (pictured) in Ipswich, England, is a pioneering example of energy-conscious design in an office building. Its grass roof, large atrium, and glass-paneled walls provide natural light and help maintain even temperatures inside the building year round.

in natural daylight. A large atrium also increased the natural daylight entering the building, so less artificial light was required. The building featured a grass roof, which kept the floors below it cool. The building became a pioneering example of energy-conscious design for a corporate office building.

In the late 1970s and into the early 1990s, scientists continued to research energy-efficient building processes. Through this research, they developed more-effective solar panels, prefabricated efficient wall systems, water reclamation systems, modular construction units, and more direct use of natural light through windows to decrease energy needs in the daytime.

Healthy Environments

During the 1980s, some architects became concerned about how buildings and building materials affected the health of the people inside them. American architect William McDonough publicly spoke about his concerns about the toxicity of materials used in commercial buildings. For example, buildings constructed prior to 1980 often had asbestos in flooring and other building materials. Asbestos is a group of six types of naturally occurring minerals. These minerals are made into fine, durable fibers and can be woven into cloth or added to cement, plastics, or other materials. If inhaled or ingested, asbestos fibers can lead to a type of cancer called mesothelioma, as well as lung cancer and other diseases. McDonough and other architects urged the construction industry

SITE DEVELOPMENT

For new construction projects, site selection is an important part of building sustainably. Where a project is located can significantly affect its environmental impact and overall sustainability. In order to minimize impact to the environment, developers' building sites should avoid land that is usable farmland, frequently floods, is a habitat for threatened or endangered species, is near wetlands, or is available for use as a public park or open space.

Instead, choosing to renovate an existing building can reduce the environmental impact of a new building project. Alternately, choosing a site for a new building that is within an existing urban community can reduce stress on the environment because necessary infrastructure such as utilities are already established. In addition, sites near residential areas and neighborhoods can shorten the commute for building occupants and allow them to take public transportation, bike, or walk to the site. A shortened commute benefits the environment by reducing fuel consumption and pollution and also improves the quality of life for building occupants. Other considerations include the availability of basic services such as schools, restaurants, libraries, and medical services. By carefully selecting a site, developers can minimize the environmental impact of the project while also benefiting the economy and community.

to look at the building processes, materials, and air systems being used in construction.

Early research looked at off-gassing materials inside buildings. Off-gassing refers to the chemical vapors released into the air during construction and by various construction materials such as plywood, fabrics, and paints. In response to the research, McDonough + Partners developed new carpets made from plants and certain woods that were chemical free for use in the renovation of the Environmental Defense Fund offices. This use of nontoxic materials has become a key component of sustainable construction.

> **WORDS IN CONTEXT**
> ___
> **off-gassing**
> The release of a chemical in the form of a gas.

The White House Goes Green

With the election of President Bill Clinton in 1992, sustainability advocates urged the White House to become an example of sustainable building. On Earth Day, April 21, 1993, Clinton announced a plan to make the White House a model for efficiency and waste reduction. The project, which included the Eisenhower Executive Office Building (formerly known as the Old Executive Office Building) across the street, began with an energy audit by the US Department of Energy. The US Environmental Protection Agency (EPA) also conducted an environmental audit of the White House. Nearly one hundred environmentalists, design professionals, engineers, and government officials worked to create energy-conservation solutions for the project, using off-the-shelf technologies and readily available sustainable products. They identified opportunities to reduce waste, lower energy use, and use renewable resources when possible, while at the same time improving air quality and building comfort.

The Greening of the White House project incorporated many changes and improvements to the nearly two-hundred-year-old building. Some of the changes implemented included using energy-saving lightbulbs and maximizing the use of natural light. Workers replaced the windows in the Eisenhower Executive Office

Building with double-paned glass windows, which better insulated the building and saved energy. They also installed energy-saving office equipment and replaced refrigerators and coolers with more-energy-efficient models. The White House started a comprehensive waste-recycling program. Even the vehicle fleet was updated by leasing vehicles that used cleaner-burning fuels. Outside the building, landscaping was updated to reduce water and pesticide use.

Within three years, the sustainable improvements saved $300,000 in annual energy and water costs, landscaping expenses, and solid-waste costs. The improvements also reduced emissions into the atmosphere by 931 tons (845 metric tons) of carbon annually. The success of the project encouraged other federal buildings to embark on their own green improvements. The Pentagon, the Presidio of San Francisco, and the US Department of Energy headquarters underwent green projects. In the 1990s the National Park Service also opened green facilities at several national parks, including the Grand Canyon, Yellowstone, and Denali.

LEED Building

By the 1990s architects interested in designing buildings that were sensitive to the environment and the community supported a concept they called "sustainable development" or "sustainability." The US Green Building Council (USGBC) was created in 1993 to promote the design and construction of buildings that are environmentally responsible, profitable, and a healthy place for occupants. The USGBC is a world leader and educator for green building and sustainable development. The organization works to integrate different sectors of the construction industry to work toward a sustainable future for all. The council consists of various trade associations, architects, designers, and others interested in sustainable construction.

In the 1990s the USGBC created a rating system for sustainability. Leadership in Energy and Environmental Design (LEED) is a system for designing, constructing, and certifying green buildings. The LEED system defines sustainable construction as architecture that uses renewable sources of energy and passive techniques for ventilation and lighting. It also incorporates, maintains, and recycles greenery, water, and waste. It uses environmentally sensitive construction techniques and fosters livable communities.

Under the LEED system, buildings can be classified as Certified, Silver, Gold, or Platinum on the basis of how they score on six building components: sustainable sites, water efficiency, energy and atmosphere, materials and resources, indoor environmental quality, and innovation and design process. Buildings earn points for these different components, such as by saving energy or being close to mass transit. The higher the point total, the more sustainable the building is.

Today LEED certification has become an internationally recognized and nationally accepted benchmark for the design, construction, and operation of sustainable, high-performance green

LIVING ROOFS

While green roofs have been around for centuries, the modern living roof emerged in the late 1970s. A green or living roof is partially or completely covered with vegetation. The living roof is made of several layers, including a growing medium planted over a waterproof membrane. Some living roofs incorporate technology to create sophisticated root barriers, drainage systems, and irrigation systems that can be additional layers on the roof.

A living roof has many benefits for the environment and building occupants. The vegetation absorbs rainwater, reducing the amount of runoff from a building. It provides insulation, keeping a building cool in the summer and warm in the winter. It also creates a habitat for plants, animals, and insects in urban environments. In addition, the vegetation on a living roof can naturally absorb carbon dioxide and other pollutants in the atmosphere and release oxygen, improving air quality for urban and suburban communities.

In urban environments a living roof can help reduce temperatures in cities. Many urban building materials absorb the sun's rays and reemit them as heat, which can make cities hotter than outlying areas. Living roofs provide shade and also remove heat from the air, reducing temperatures on the roof surface and surrounding air.

buildings. LEED ratings give building designers and owners information they need to have an immediate and measurable effect on their building's performance and sustainability. There are five different LEED rating systems, each designed for a specific type of building project, from new construction to improvements for existing buildings.

Seattle's Bullitt Center

Opened in 2013 in Seattle, Washington, the Bullitt Center is an example of cutting edge sustainable construction. The six-story office building features twenty-six 400-foot-deep (122-m) geothermal wells drilled beneath the building to provide heating and cooling delivered through radiant systems. A computer manages the building's temperature, opening and closing blinds as needed, and triple-glazed windows provide insulation and can also be opened for ventilation.

On the roof, a massive array of solar panels delivers electricity to the building. The majority of lighting comes from natural light, while electricity use is kept low through an internal system that gives each tenant a specific energy budget. If tenants use less than their allotted amount, they can trade with other building tenants who may need more energy. Tenants are invested in the building's energy success. When the building meets its energy budget, tenants pay nothing for electricity.

The building harvests its own rainwater in a 56,000-gallon (211,983-L) cistern. After filtration and treatment, the harvested rainwater can supply 100 percent of the building's water needs, including drinking water. Water from sinks and showers gets filtered and put back into the earth. Special composting toilets barely use any water and eventually produce compost that can be used as a natural fertilizer.

In April 2015 the Bullitt Center was designated as a Living Building, as certified by the International Living Future Institute. A Living Building must meet twenty design criteria in seven performance areas—site, water, energy, health, materials, equity, and beauty. It must also be net-zero energy and net-zero water for twelve months of occupancy. A net-zero building uses approximately the same amount of energy or water that it generates on-site annually. Around the world only ten other buildings have been awarded Living Building Status. "That's a significant achievement for a six-story, Class A office building," says Alex Wilson, the founding editor of BuildingGreen. "Particularly in one of the most challenging climates in the country for solar energy."[5]

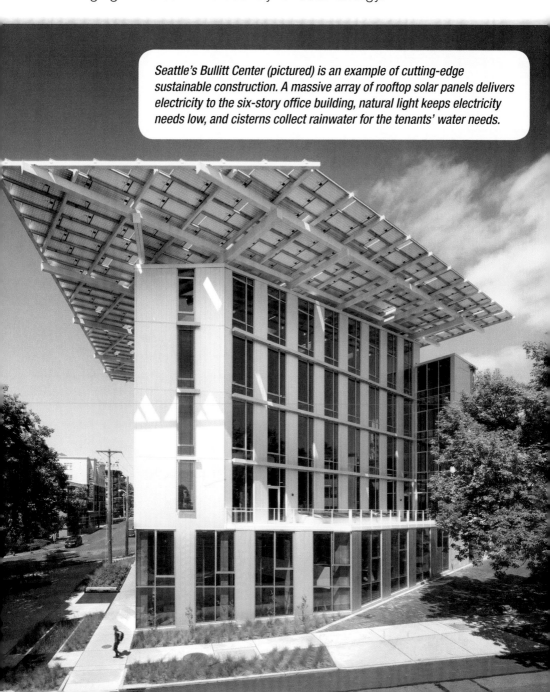

Seattle's Bullitt Center (pictured) is an example of cutting-edge sustainable construction. A massive array of rooftop solar panels delivers electricity to the six-story office building, natural light keeps electricity needs low, and cisterns collect rainwater for the tenants' water needs.

Bullitt Foundation president and chief executive officer Denis Hayes was the driving force behind the vision for the Bullitt Center. Today he says that the building is fully leased and cash positive, taking in more cash than it expends. Tenants are actively engaged in meeting energy and water use goals and working sustainably. "Today's living buildings, like the Bullitt Center, represent efforts to learn from nature how to exist comfortably and productively in a particular environment, making the least possible demand on resources,"[6] says Hayes.

The Future of Sustainable Construction

Today research to improve sustainable construction and green building is being done around the world by national laboratories, private companies, universities, and industry groups. Through their study on energy and atmosphere research, materials and resources, indoor environmental quality, and other topics, scientists are making exciting contributions to the future of sustainable construction.

CHAPTER TWO

Using Energy Efficiently

> "Improving the design of buildings to reduce the demand of energy is essential in trying to achieve net-zero energy requirements for new projects."

—Michael Peachey, architect at MW Architects Inc.

Michael Peachey, "Expert Advice on Sustainable Home Architecture: An Interview with Michael Peachey of MW Architects Inc.," Southern California Homes, 2016. www.southerncaliforniahomes.com.

According to the US Energy Information Administration, about 40 percent of total US energy consumption occurred in residential and commercial buildings in 2015. Common uses of energy include heating, water heating, air-conditioning, lighting, refrigeration, cooking, and running a variety of appliances and other equipment.

All energy consumption has some impact on the environment, such as air and water pollution, damage to public health, wildlife and habitat loss, water depletion, land degradation, and emissions that contribute to global warming. Fossil fuels such as coal, oil, and natural gas generally do more harm to the environment than renewable energy sources such as wind, solar, or geothermal energy. By using energy more efficiently and using more renewable energy, sustainable construction designs can reduce the amount of fuel needed to generate electricity and thus the amount of greenhouse gases and other pollution emitted into the air.

Using Sensor Technology

Many building-control systems do not have access to specific information about energy usage. As a result, they may waste energy by heating or cooling parts of the building that do not need to be heated or cooled. One way to provide more information is to incorporate advanced sensors and controls into buildings. Studies have shown that using advanced sensors and controls can reduce energy consumption by 20 to 30 percent. Sensors collect data such as outside air and room temperatures, humidity, levels of light, and pollutants. "It is widely accepted that energy-consuming systems such as heating, ventilating, and air conditioning (HVAC) units in buildings are under, or poorly, controlled causing them to waste energy," says Patrick Hughes, director of the US Department of Energy's Oak Ridge National Laboratory (ORNL) Building Technologies Program. "Buildings could increase their energy efficiency if control systems had access to additional information."[7]

However, many current sensor systems are expensive because they must be wired into a building's electrical system, which can be a challenging and time-consuming task. Additionally, the sensors can be costly. For instance, some wireless nodes cost $150 to $300 per node. Each wireless node gathers and processes sensory information and communicates it to other nodes in the system. To address this problem, scientists at ORNL are developing an innovative, low-cost, wireless sensor technology to help small commercial buildings become more energy efficient. The new wireless sensor prototype costs only $1 to $10 per node. Scientists are able to reduce the cost of the nodes by using advanced manufacturing techniques such as additive roll-to-roll manufacturing. This technique allows manufacturers to print electronics components such as circuits, sensors, antennae, and photovoltaic cells and batteries on flexible plastic base materials. Then the wireless nodes can be easily installed using a peel-and-stick adhesive backing instead of being hardwired into the system. The wireless smart sensors collect data about the conditions inside a building and send it to a receiver, which compiles information from many nodes and uses it to adjust the building's energy-consuming systems. The more and better information received from the wireless nodes, the better the building can manage its energy consumption. While the technology is still in the developmental phase, both new and existing buildings will be able to use the wireless smart sensor technology. "This technology provides the information that enables ongoing continuous commissioning, fault detection and diagnosis, and service organization notifications when needed, ensuring optimal building system operations throughout their service life,"[8] says ORNL's Teja Kuruganti, a principal investigator on the low-cost wireless sensors project.

Heating and Cooling Systems

In buildings, heating and cooling systems consume significant amounts of energy and can produce large amounts of pollution. According to the US Department of Energy, heating and cooling systems account for about half of a typical American home's energy

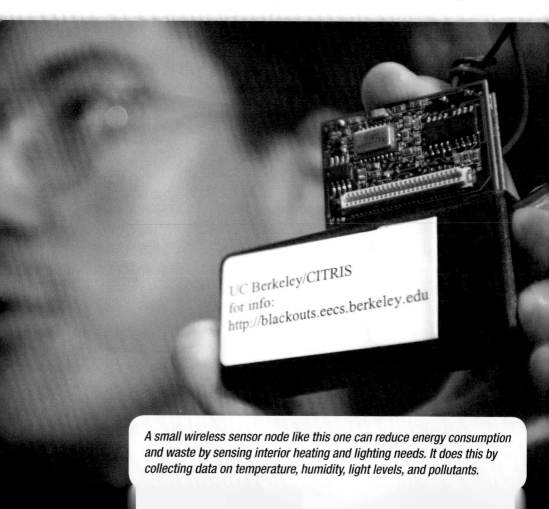

UC Berkeley/CITRIS
for info:
http://blackouts.eecs.berkeley.edu

A small wireless sensor node like this one can reduce energy consumption and waste by sensing interior heating and lighting needs. It does this by collecting data on temperature, humidity, light levels, and pollutants.

use, making it the largest energy expense for most homes. The amount of energy a home or building uses varies depending on the climate in which it is located as well as the type of heating and cooling systems installed and the level of insulation.

Reducing energy use in heating and cooling systems is one way to make a building more sustainable. Scientists are investigating how advanced energy-efficiency controls can be used to reduce energy consumption. In 2014 scientists with the US Department of Energy's Pacific Northwest National Laboratory conducted a yearlong trial of these advanced controls installed at malls, grocery stores, and other buildings. They found that commercial buildings using these controls could reduce heating and cooling electricity use by an average of 57 percent. "We've long known that heating and cooling are among the biggest energy consumers in buildings, largely because most buildings don't use sophisticated controls," says the study's lead researcher, engineer Srinivas Katipamula. "But our tests of controls installed at real, working commercial buildings clearly demonstrate how much more energy efficient air-conditioning systems can be."[9]

For many commercial buildings, a large metal box on the roof holds the HVAC unit. Factory-packaged HVAC units often run for hours, even if not needed, because they do not monitor building conditions and rarely receive maintenance. Inefficient HVAC systems often lead to higher power bills and add to greenhouse gas emissions by requiring more electricity to run, which in turn releases more carbon dioxide into the atmosphere.

The researchers took sophisticated, energy-efficiency controls from more expensive HVAC units and adapted them for the packaged rooftop units. They used sensors and variable-speed motors to automatically adjust their operations on the basis of the conditions inside and outside a building. The controls determine when to run ventilation fans and how fast to run them. They sense if the unit can use cold air from outside to cool a building instead of using mechanically cooled indoor air. The researchers found that the HVAC units using the advanced control systems could cut energy use from 20 percent to 90 percent, with larger buildings that used larger HVAC units saving the most energy.

An office air-conditioning unit undergoes repairs. Heating, ventilation, and air-conditioning (HVAC) units are notoriously inefficient. Many run around the clock, resulting in high energy bills and more greenhouse gas emissions.

"I'm proud to see the advanced controls my colleagues and I evaluated not only work in the real world, but produce significant energy savings," says Katipamula. "We hope commercial building owners will be inspired by these tangible savings and install advanced controls in their rooftop HVAC units."[10]

Other scientists are working on new systems that can adjust the room temperature in buildings, which reduces the need for air-conditioning or heating and reduces overall energy use. At the Institute of Advanced Technology at the Universiti Putra Malaysia, a team of researchers created a system called Nanotechnology for Encapsulation of Phase Change Material (NPCM) that reduces room temperatures. Phase change materials are substances that melt and solidify at a certain temperature and are able to store

BUILDING ORIENTATION

Passive techniques to control a building's climate can reduce the energy used for heating and cooling. These techniques include the use of building orientation, shading devices, natural ventilation, and operable facades. For example, building orientation is the practice of positioning a building so that its location and design maximize its surroundings. To reduce energy consumption for heating and cooling, builders can orient buildings to use free energy from sunlight.

In the Northern Hemisphere, a building with passive solar heating would be oriented so that its windows face the south to absorb the maximum amount of the sun's energy. In the Southern Hemisphere, that building would be oriented so that its windows face north. Even during winter, a building with passive solar heating can stay warm. Insulated windows help keep the heat in the building after the sun sets. In the summer months, shading systems or an overhang can keep the building cool. Using these strategies when building can significantly reduce heating and cooling costs and environmental impact.

and release large amounts of thermal energy. Phase change materials include certain salt hydrates, eutectics (a mixture whose melting point is lower than that of any other mixture of the same materials), and some polymers with long chain molecules composed primarily of carbon and hydrogen. When these materials freeze, they release large amounts of energy in the form of heat. When the materials melt, an equal amount of heat energy is absorbed from the environment. Dr. Mohd Zobir Hussein, head of the research team, explains:

> This NPCM method is the first of its kind in Malaysia that can absorb, store and release thermal heat when the surrounding temperature where the material is located is above or below melting temperature. These properties allow the phase change material to store the thermal energy when it melts and releases the energy when it solidifies. . . . If it is used as [a] passive or active building component, it can help in controlling the internal building temperature fluctuations which will result in thermal-comfort buildings.[11]

According to researchers, NPCM substances can be added into cement or paint as active insulation materials and applied to a building's ceilings or walls. If added to building components, the NPCM materials will not have any adverse effects on the building's structural integrity.

Maximizing Energy Performance

Other research to improve the sustainability of construction involves ways to maximize the performance of lighting, appliances, and other energy-consuming equipment in order to decrease the amount of energy that a building uses. Across the United States and the world, traditional incandescent lightbulbs are being replaced by more energy-efficient light-emitting diode (LED) lightbulbs. LED lightbulbs can last several years longer than incandescent lightbulbs because they do not have a tungsten filament that burns out quickly. According to the US Department of Energy, switching to LED lighting could save the United States an estimated $250 billion in energy costs over a twenty-year period by reducing the amount of electricity needed to illuminate the lightbulbs by nearly 50 percent. In addition, the switch to LED lighting would eliminate 1,984 million tons (1,800 million metric tons) of carbon emissions over the same period.

However, many current LED lightbulbs are made with rare-earth elements such as cerium, europium, gadolinium, lanthanum, terbium, and yttrium that are in high demand for use in other high-tech devices, which increases the cost of LED lighting. To make a lower-cost LED lighting option, researchers at Rutgers University reported in 2014 that they had designed a family of materials that used copper iodide, the elements of which are more abundant. In addition to being readily available, the copper iodide materials were able to glow a warm white shade using an inexpensive process. "Combining these features, this material class shows significant promise for use in general lighting applications,"[12] the scientists say.

> **WORDS IN CONTEXT**
>
> **compound**
>
> A substance made from atoms of two or more different elements that are joined together by chemical bonds.

Other scientists are working on ways to make a building's windows more energy efficient. In a 2013 article in the journal *Solar Energy Materials & Solar Cells*, Ben Hatton, an engineering professor at the University of Toronto, and his research team at Harvard University described a process they developed to reduce heat loss in the winter and keep buildings cool in the summer. Hatton noted that windows account for about 40 percent of a building's energy losses, and therefore costs. He turned to nature to find a solution, as he explains:

> In contrast to man-made thermal control systems, living organisms have evolved an entirely different and highly efficient mechanism to control temperature that is based on the design of internal vascular networks. For example, blood vessels dilate to increase blood flow close to the skin surface to increase convective heat transfer, whereas they constrict and limit flow when our skin is exposed to cold.[13]

Using this idea, the researchers designed optically clear, flexible elastomer sheets that had miniature channels running through them. Elastomer is a natural or synthetic chemical compound that has elastic properties, such as rubber. Room-temperature water was pumped through the channels. When the researchers attached the elastomer sheets to regular glass window panes, laboratory tests found that using the sheets resulted in a cooling of 12.5°F to 16°F (7°C to 9°C). "Our results show that an artificial vascular network within a transparent layer, composed of channels on the micrometer to millimeter scale, and extending over the surface of a window, offers an additional and novel cooling mechanism for building windows and a new thermal control tool for building design,"[14] says Hatton.

Managing Plug Loads

Other energy-efficient research is focusing on plug load, or the energy used by appliances that are powered with an ordinary AC plug. As consumer electronics have become more common and complex, the number of devices plugged in to AC outlets is increasing, which is also driving up energy use. Many of these devices never turn off completely. Instead, they continue to draw a small amount of power, even when not in use, so that they will be ready to start quickly when activated by a user.

According to the US Department of Energy, plug loads consume approximately one-third of the energy in US commercial buildings and are expected to grow to 35 percent of total building energy use by 2025 as the number of devices increases. Devices that contribute to plug load do not fall into traditional HVAC, lighting, or large-appliance categories. Examples of plug load devices include everyday entertainment and household devices such as personal computers, laptops, televisions, and personal devices. In commercial buildings, information processing, medical equipment, and food service equipment also fall into the plug load category.

In 2012 the General Services Administration's (GSA) Green Proving Ground program assessed the effectiveness of advanced power strips to manage plug load energy use. In eight GSA buildings where plug loads averaged 21 percent, researchers replaced twelve standard power strips with advanced power strips, which monitored energy use and provided power to a variety of devices over three separate four-week test periods.

The program assessed three energy-reduction strategies. Some power strips were able to schedule timer control, enabling users to set days and times when an electrical circuit would turn on and off. Others incorporated load-sensing control, which monitored a specific device's power state (master) and turned off auxiliary devices when the master's power consumption fell below a set threshold. A third set of advanced power strips used a combination of the two methods. The researchers found that the scheduled timer control was most effective at reducing energy consumption, resulting in an average electricity savings of 48 percent. The most energy savings occurred in areas with devices such as printers, copiers, coffeemakers, and water coolers, which were powered twenty-four hours per day. "Plug loads are an increasingly large portion of building energy profiles. Managing those loads is key to making federal buildings energy efficient,"[15] says John Remis, the facility services manager at the Richmond (Virginia) Federal Building.

Solar Energy: A Renewable Energy Source

Sustainable construction also incorporates renewable energy sources, technologies designed to capture energy from natural, nonpolluting sources such as the sun, wind, geothermal sources, and water. Using renewable energy to supply a building's power needs can reduce dependence on nonrenewable fossil fuels and the pollution related to the extraction, transportation, and use of these fuels. Some buildings incorporate solar panels to collect energy from the sun and turn it into electricity or use it to heat water. Solar thermal systems contain water that flows through the panels and is heated by the sun, which provides hot water to the building. Other solar panels use many photovoltaic cells linked together that react with sunlight and generate a flow of electricity. Metal conductive plates on the sides of the photovoltaic cells collect the flow of electrons and transfer them to wires that can immediately deliver the electricity to the building.

Some scientists are working on ways to improve solar panels for buildings. Most solar panels used in homes and commercial buildings are made using thick layers of material to absorb sunlight. While thicker layers work best, they are expensive. Lower-cost designs that use thinner layers of light-absorbing materials do not extract enough energy. In a 2013 study from an international team of scientists from the United Kingdom, Belgium, China, and Japan, researchers demonstrated that solar panels could be improved by up to 22 percent by covering their surface with aluminum studs, which at a microscopic level look like interlocking LEGO building bricks. These aluminum studs bend and trap light inside the absorbing material. The research team attached rows of aluminum cylinders that measured only 100 nanometers across the top of a solar panel. In comparison, a sheet of paper is about 100,000 nanometers thick. The cylinders interacted with passing sunlight, bending and scat-

tering individual light rays and causing them to change direction. As the rays became trapped inside the solar panel and traveled for longer distances through its layer of absorbing material, more energy could be extracted. Lead author Nicholas Hylton from the Department of Physics at Imperial College London explains:

> In recent years both the efficiency and cost of commercial solar panels have improved but they remain expensive compared to fossil fuels. As the absorbing material alone can make up half the cost of a solar panel our aim has been to reduce to a minimum the amount that is needed. The success of our technology, in combination with modern anti-reflection coatings, will take us a long way down the path towards highly efficient and thin solar cells that could be available at a competitive price.[16]

Improving Solar Reliability and Effectiveness

Other researchers are working on ways to make solar panels more reliable and effective. One of the challenges of using solar panels is that over time, corrosion can harm the panels' electronics and connections, decreasing the amount of electricity the panels can produce. Solar panels in regions where higher temperatures or humidity commonly occur often corrode at faster rates than those in cooler, less humid areas. Scientists at Sandia National Laboratories are studying the effects of corrosion to help develop longer-lasting and more reliable solar panels. To do so, researchers use environmental chambers to speed up the corroding effects of temperature, humidity, pollutants, and salt water on electronics and other solar panel components. Eric Schindelholz, a Sandia National Laboratories materials reliability researcher, explains:

> One of our primary goals is to predict how fast corrosion will occur and what damage it does, given certain environments and materials. This, in turn, gives us information to select the right materials for design or to develop materials for corrosion-resistance for a particular environment. It also allows us to assess the health and operational risk of systems as they age. This is especially important for solar energy systems, which are susceptible to corrosion but are expected to last for decades.[17]

Erik Spoerke, a researcher in Sandia's Electronic, Optical and Nano Materials Department, is working on developing new nanocomposite films that could block corrosion entirely. When used as layers within the solar cell, the nanocomposite films act as a barrier against water vapor and corrosive gases. The films, which can be 100 times thinner than a human hair, will help pro-

WORDS IN CONTEXT

corrosion

The deterioration of a metal as a result of chemical reactions between it and the surrounding environment.

GEOTHERMAL ENERGY

Geothermal energy is a renewable energy produced from the heat stored in the water beneath the earth's surface. Scientists and engineers have developed three main technologies to extract and use earth's heat: geothermal electricity generation, geothermal heat pumps, and high-temperature geothermal heating.

Geothermal power plants convert the thermal energy in underground reservoirs of hot water and steam into electricity. Unlike fossil fuel power plants, geothermal power plants do not burn fuel or have smoky emissions. Instead, they use hot water and steam to run electric generators. Geothermal power plants can then send electricity via power lines to consumers.

Geothermal heat pumps can be used to heat and cool homes and businesses. A few feet below its surface, the earth remains a relatively constant temperature year-round, approximately 50°F to 60°F (10°C to 15.6°C). During the winter months, the heat pump removes heat from the ground through a heat exchanger. It pumps the heat through an indoor air-delivery system. During the warmer summer months, the heat pump transfers heat from indoor air to the heat exchanger.

Direct geothermal heating systems pipe hot water just under the earth's surface through a series of pipes to houses and buildings. Heat exchangers extract the heat from the hot water and transfer it to a secondary fluid. This fluid then circulates through a home, building, or other structure in a closed loop, providing heat. After it passes through the pipes, the geothermal water returns to the underground reservoir. There it is reheated and ready to use again.

tect solar cells from corrosion. Spoerke's team is experimenting with inexpensive combinations of inorganic compounds and organic polymers to make the films. According to Spoerke, the combinations must be designed and mixed carefully. "It's about assembling those structures in the right way so that you can use inexpensive materials and still get the benefits you want,"[18] he says.

Through research in a variety of areas, from solar energy to wireless building sensors, scientists are developing ways for buildings to use energy resources more efficiently. These advances are just one way they are making construction more sustainable.

CHAPTER THREE

Building with Sustainable Materials

> **"Using appropriate materials and designs for each climate and paying careful attention to the details throughout the construction process, any style of house can be green."**

—Carl Seville, cofounder of SK Collaborative, a green building firm

Quoted in Massachusetts Contractors Academy, "Expert Interview with Carl Seville of SK Collaborative on Residential Green Building," July 27, 2015. www.247mass.com.

The construction industry uses large amounts of raw materials, such as sand, gravel, fabric, foam, concrete, metals, and lumber. Some of these materials are finite resources. For example, sand is a primary ingredient in cement and building concrete, is used to make glass, and is also used in roads and massive land reclamation projects. The world's supply of sand that can be used for construction is dwindling, and it takes hundreds of thousands of years to replenish it. Rapid urbanization around the world has increased the demand for sand. Sand miners are digging deeper, disrupting sensitive ecosystems in the hunt for sand.

In addition, the extraction of raw materials such as sand, gravel, and certain woods can seriously damage the environment, cause a loss of habitats, and threaten nearby ecosystems. Extracting, processing, and transporting these materials releases large amounts of carbon dioxide and other greenhouse gases into the atmosphere. And despite the long life of buildings, the eventual demolition or redevelopment of a building site can produce significant waste for disposal.

To preserve the earth's scarce natural resources and make building more sustainable, architects, engineers, environmentalists, scientists, and others are working to develop and use materials and resources that are environmentally friendly, sustainably sourced, and readily available.

Sustainable Materials

Materials used in sustainable construction preserve natural resources. Preservation happens by using renewable materials such as crops or using reclaimed or recycled materials instead of new ones. Architects can design projects to use fewer total materials. Creating less waste in the construction process and avoiding the use of scarce, nonrenewable materials can also preserve natural resources.

The construction industry can also reduce the impact on the environment by using materials that require less energy to extract, process, and manufacture. Reducing the distance materials need to be transported can decrease the related problems of fuel use, emissions, and traffic. Preventing waste from going to landfills is another way to reduce construction's impact on the environment. And from the beginning of a project, designing and building so that materials can be easily reused and recycled at the end of the building's life cycle is another part of sustainable construction. By considering the product's entire life cycle, the construction industry can identify ways to reduce environmental impact, conserve natural resources, and reduce costs.

> **WORDS IN CONTEXT**
>
> **reclaimed**
> Retrieved from an original use and repurposed for another use.

Reusing Existing Building Stock

Instead of building a new structure, in many cases an existing building can be renovated for a different use. In a 2012 report by the Preservation Green Lab titled "The Greenest Building: Quantifying the Environmental Value of Building Reuse," researchers found that reusing and renovating existing buildings offered environmental savings between 4 percent and 46 percent over demolishing old structures and building new ones when comparing buildings with the same energy-performance level. In the report, researchers cited the city of Portland, Oregon, as an example, saying that if Portland "were to retrofit and reuse the single-family homes and commercial office buildings that it is otherwise likely to demolish over the next 10 years, the potential impact reduction would total approximately 231,000 metric tons of CO_2—approximately 15 percent of their county's total CO_2 reduction targets over the next decade."[19]

When Wieden + Kennedy, an international advertising agency, searched for a space for the company's Portland, Oregon,

Researchers say that demolition of single-family homes and other buildings adds significant amounts of carbon dioxide to the atmosphere. Reuse and renovation of older structures can actually reduce greenhouse gas emissions.

headquarters in 1999, it chose a building built in 1908. The old building spread across one square block in Portland's Pearl District, a warehouse and railroad district. The building was originally constructed as a paint warehouse for the Fuller Brush Company. Later it was insulated with 6 inches (15.2 cm) of cork and turned into a cold-storage warehouse. Years of use for cold-storage led to extensive wood rot and other structural damage. Eventually, the warehouse was abandoned and sat unused for decades.

In 1999 Wieden + Kennedy chose to invest $36 million in remodeling the space for its headquarters. The existing masonry and timber-frame structure was renovated into offices for the agency's four hundred designers and support staff, along with several non-profit arts organizations. The sustainable construction featured reuse of the building's original structural timbers and an under-floor air-distribution system. It also used a variety of reclaimed resources throughout the building, including the reuse of beams for the wood flooring. Much of the building's lighting comes from natural light entering through massive skylights and expansive windows.

These sustainable features helped the building win the Energy Efficiency BEST award from the City of Portland. The renovation was also a catalyst for the redevelopment of other historic buildings in the city's Pearl District. Additionally, the renovation of the warehouse earned it a spot on the National Register of Historic Places.

Using Recycled Materials

Sustainable construction uses recycled building materials as much as possible. Using recycled materials reduces the need for natural raw materials and decreases construction waste. Builders can use salvaged and refurbished light fixtures, doors, cabinets, and flooring whenever possible. Early in the building process, designers and builders should discuss material selection and the availability of recycled materials. Factors such as cost, availability, distance to transport, ease of installation, the effects of harvesting new materials, and the effects on local

> **WORDS IN CONTEXT**
>
> **refurbished**
> Renovated and made useable again.

economies should all be considered when selecting sustainable materials. For example, if a recycled material must be shipped from halfway around the world, the transportation costs and pollution caused by transport may offset any benefits gained from using the repurposed materials.

Many common building products are made from recycled materials. Drywall, steel, and acoustical ceilings are some of the products made from recycled materials. Some materials are made from postconsumer recycled content, which is waste from items that people have already used, such as aluminum cans or glass. Other building products are made with preconsumer recycled content, which is waste produced by the product-manufacturing process, such as scraps from steel manufacturing.

Scientists are developing new ways to incorporate recycled materials into building projects. They are using recycled rubber in flooring, recycled paper in cabinets, and recycled glass or porcelain from old toilets in countertops. Wall insulation can even be made from old jeans.

At Rutgers University, assistant research professor Thomas Nosker and his colleagues invented a structural plastic lumber, a material made from milk containers, coffee cups, and other recycled plastics. The plastic lumber is lighter than steel, longer lasting than lumber, and strong enough to support 120-ton (109-metric-ton) locomotives. "People complain about plastics because they don't degrade," says Nosker. "We found a way to turn that to our advantage with a product."[20]

Three decades ago, Nosker became interested in finding a use for the mounting piles of discarded plastic containers that were ending up in landfills. One of the most difficult types of plastic waste to deal with was high-density polyethylene (HDPE), the plastic used to make milk containers. At first Nosker and his team tried to make the milk containers into a substitute for chemically treated wood for park benches and docks. But the recycled HDPE planks sagged over time. The team tried combining HDPE with other plastics, without success. Then Nosker stumbled on the right mix of plastic. "We combined HDPE with polystyrene from old Big Mac containers,"[21] Nosker says. When combined in specific proportions, the tiny plastic particles interlock, causing the blended plastics to gain strength.

Now that they had the formula to create strong, recycled plastics, Nosker and his team decided to use them to build objects traditionally made of wood. For centuries, wood lumber has been used in construction. Although it is durable, flexible, and generally affordable, wood lumber has some drawbacks. To protect the wood from insects, animals, and weather, it is often treated with toxic preservatives that can leak into the surrounding soil, water,

Recycled plastic lumber (pictured) has become popular in environmentally sensitive areas. Bridges, boat docks, and picnic tables are among the structures that have been built from plastic lumber.

and groundwater. Structural recycled plastic lumber does not need to be treated with toxic preservatives, eliminating this risk.

Today recycled plastic lumber is growing popular in environmentally sensitive areas, particularly where railroads cross streams. Bridges built from the material can be found in New Jersey's Pine Barrens, as well as California, Maine, Ohio, Scotland, and other areas. The structural plastic lumber is also being used to build docks, picnic tables, park benches, and other structures worldwide. In the United States it has been used to make about 1.5 million railway ties. Recycling the plastic into the railway ties means that about 300 million pounds (136 million kg) of plastic waste will not be sent to landfills, harm marine life, or litter beaches with debris.

Improving Traditional Building Materials

Concrete has shaped many of world's buildings and structures; it is used in schools, houses, roads, bridges, tunnels, and more. Concrete is actually the most commonly used human-made material in the world. According to the World Business Council for Sustainable Development, twice as much concrete is used worldwide than the total of all other building materials, including wood, steel, plastic, and aluminum. Concrete's strength, durability, thermal mass, and affordability make it the top choice for many construction projects.

The production of concrete—and in particular its primary ingredient, cement—can be very environmentally unfriendly. Almost every step in its production, from mining and transporting to heating with fossil fuels in a kiln, emits carbon dioxide and other emissions into the atmosphere. According to the World Business Council for Sustainable Development, concrete production is responsible for 5 percent of global carbon dioxide emissions. In addition, the extraction of raw materials at mines produces noise and dust in local communities. And because water is an ingredient

> **WORDS IN CONTEXT**
>
> **thermal mass**
>
> The ability of a material to absorb and store heat energy.

TURNING PLASTIC BAGS INTO BRICKS

Danish student Lise Fuglsang Vestergaard is working on a project to convert soft plastic waste into bricks. During a stay in India to develop a refuse collection system, Vestergaard noticed that although people in India collect waste for recycling stations, they typically leave soft plastic waste, such as plastic bags, behind because it is difficult to recycle. As a result, this type of waste is becoming a growing problem in India. At the same time, Vestergaard noticed the region's clay-brick houses were almost washed away during the country's monsoon season. She decided to see if there was a way to use the plastic to make bricks that could withstand the monsoon rains, solving both problems.

Vestergaard experimented with melting the plastic and eventually developed a process to transform the plastic into bricks. First the plastic waste is collected and washed, if needed. Then it is ground into small pieces. The plastic particles are then stuffed into a mold and put in a solar grill, which uses the sun's energy to melt the plastic. Once the melted plastic cools, it can be removed from the mold as a plastic brick. In addition, the bricks have two holes that allow them to be stacked and connected with bamboo poles, creating more stable walls without other building materials. Once built into walls, the plastic bricks can be covered with a layer of clay, which protects the plastic from the sun. When the monsoon rains come, the plastic bricks are more durable than all-clay bricks.

in concrete, people living in areas where water is scarce may have to compete with concrete production for resources.

Scientists are working on several ways to make concrete more sustainable. In Australia the construction company Wagners created earth-friendly concrete (EFC) that uses blast furnace slag, an industrial waste from steel production, and fly ash, a waste from coal power generation, instead of portland cement, the most common type of cement used around the world. By replacing 100 percent of the portland cement in the concrete, Wagners EFC reduces carbon emissions by an estimated 90 percent while retaining about the same cost. The EFC concrete has been used to build the taxiway and turning node at Brisbane's airport.

In Malaysia, researchers are investigating the use of dried sewage sludge as an alternative to cement in concrete. The disposal of sludge from sewage water treatment is a growing problem for Malaysian wastewater plants. Stricter environmental regulations have banned the practice of burying sludge in soil because of its high heavy metal content that could harm the environment, leaving the wastewater plants looking for disposal options. Researchers from Universiti Teknologi MARA are investigating the potential of using this sludge to replace cement in concrete production. To test the idea, the researchers mixed dried domestic waste sludge powder (DWSP) with cement to produce different types of concrete. They compared each concrete mixture with traditional concrete, comparing compressive strength, water absorption, water permeability, and permeability to salt. "Overall, there is potential for using DWSP as a partial cement replacement. However, more detailed research should be conducted to yield methods for producing quality powder,"[22] the researchers concluded.

Recycling Concrete

Other researchers are investigating ways to reuse and recycle concrete. Materials around the world, from aluminum cans to glass bottles, are recycled and used in new products. A team of researchers from the University of Notre Dame wants to do the same with concrete, recycling concrete from deteriorating buildings and infrastructure for use in new buildings and structures. Says Yahya Kurama, a professor of civil and environmental engineering and earth sciences, who is leading the research effort:

> **WORDS IN CONTEXT**
>
> **aggregates**
> Material formed from a loosely compacted mass of particles or fragments.

While concrete is the most commonly used construction material on earth, it is also the biggest in terms of environmental impact. Coarse aggregates, such as crushed rock and gravel, make up most of a given concrete volume. The mining, processing and transportation operations for these aggregates consume large amounts of energy and adversely affect the ecology of forested areas and riverbeds.[23]

One of the biggest barriers to using recycled concrete is the variability in the quality and properties of the material. Because of this variability, uncertainty exists about its strength, stiffness, and durability. Kurama's team is studying how using recycled concrete affects the performance of reinforced concrete structures. The team also studied a structure's deflection behavior, or how much it would deform over a long period of use under normal conditions. Kurama explains:

> We are also looking at durability and life-cycle cost, in comparison with natural aggregates, and effects of recycled concrete aggregates in pre-stressed concrete. Because of the knowledge gap to date, the use of recycled aggregates in the U.S. has been limited mostly to non-structural applications such as sidewalks and roadways, even though the quality of the material is generally significantly higher than is required in these applications. Our ultimate goal is to develop the necessary engineering background and methods for the wider utilization of recycled concrete aggregates in structural concrete, such as in buildings.[24]

Rapidly Renewable Resources

In some cases it is not possible or feasible to use recycled materials. Using materials that are made from readily renewable sources can reduce the depletion of nonrenewable and slow-to-replenish resources. Rapidly renewable materials have a regeneration rate of ten years or less. Bamboo and cork are two of the most commonly used rapidly renewable materials. For example, bamboo stalks can grow to full height in only three to five years, while an oak tree may grow for twenty years before it is mature enough to cut down and use. Bamboo can be used in many materials, including flooring, cabinets, veneers, plywood, and even concrete reinforcing.

Other rapidly renewable resources that can be used in sustainable construction include wood for carpet pads and carpets, cotton for insulation, cork in flooring, and agrifibers like wheat

Because bamboo can grow to full height in only three to five years, it is considered a rapidly renewable building material. For this reason, bamboo is being used more often in flooring and furniture.

stalks in wood-based building materials. Some building materials made from agricultural waste by-products, such as wheat straw and sugarcane bagasse or fiber crops such as kenaf and hemp, are also becoming more common. Because sunlight is the primary energy source for these materials, these products may require less energy to produce. However, energy use for processing and transportation, sometimes from remote areas, should be considered in any sustainability evaluation. In addition, because the use of rapidly renewable materials is fairly new, the long-term performance of these products is unknown.

Scientists at Armstrong Flooring have developed bio-flooring products that are both visually attractive and sustainable. BBT Bio-Flooring is made with 85 percent limestone and a patented bio-based polyester binder that is partly composed of rapidly renewable domestic corn and 40 percent recycled content. In addition to the flooring being more environmentally friendly, the scientists found that using the bio-based polyester binder actually improved the strength of the limestone-based tile. Tests showed that BBT Bio-Flooring better resists impact and cracking than standard tile. "A lot of times when people make 'green products,'

CONVERTING FOOTSTEPS INTO ELECTRICITY

Sustainable flooring can be made from bamboo, cork, or any number of sustainable materials. However, flooring may become even more sustainable, thanks to the efforts of engineers from University of Wisconsin–Madison who have developed an inexpensive, simple method to convert footsteps into electricity. The researchers used wood pulp, a common waste material of several industries. When the pulp's cellulose nanofibers are chemically treated, they produce an electrical charge when they come into contact with untreated nanofibers. When embedded in flooring, the pulp's nanofibers come into contact with the untreated nanofibers via the weight of a person's footsteps on the flooring, which in turn produces electricity that can be used to charge batteries or power lights.

In places with heavy floor traffic, such as hallways or public buildings, researchers believe that this type of technology could create significant amounts of energy. And because wood pulp is a cheap, abundant, and renewable waste product, researchers point out that the flooring could be very affordable. "We've been working a lot on harvesting energy from human activities. One way is to build something to put on people, and another way is to build something that has constant access to people. The ground is the most-used place," says researcher Xudong Wang.

Quoted in Will Cushman, "Move Over, Solar: The Next Big Renewable Energy Source Could Be at Our Feet," University of Wisconsin–Madison, October 20, 2016. http://news.wisc.edu.

they take away some of the functionality, but we actually made a green product that's two-and-a-half times the strength of our regular products," says Amy Costello, Armstrong Flooring's sustainability manager. "Not only did we reduce its environmental footprint, but we made the product better."[25] Armstrong Flooring says that its scientists will continue to research new options for sustainable flooring materials as the technology for bio-based products improves.

Recycling Construction Waste

Studies show that construction waste and demolition of structures account for over 40 percent of the total waste deposited in America's landfills. Landfills are a threat to human health and the environment. As waste in a landfill degrades, it can release several toxic gases into the atmosphere. One of the most harmful gases released is methane, which is naturally produced during the decay of organic matter. Methane is a potent greenhouse gas and has been linked to global warming. People living near landfills are at risk of heart and lung diseases from inhaling the toxic gases. In addition, toxins from decaying landfill waste can pollute groundwater, contaminating local waterways and harming local plant and animal life.

Responsible management of this waste is an important part of sustainable construction. Managing waste means eliminating or minimizing waste where possible and reusing materials that would become waste. Much of the waste from a construction project can be recycled or decreased with planning. Reducing construction waste also saves builders money by reducing dumping fees and generating revenue from the sale of recyclable waste. Reducing the amount of construction waste can also decrease pollution from construction activities. With careful planning from design to demolition, sustainable construction can create structures with sustainable materials that balance the needs of communities and the environment.

CHAPTER FOUR

Improving Indoor Air Quality

> **"Indoor air quality is the biggest health offender in homes today."**
>
> —Lisa Beres, certified green building professional
>
> Quoted in ICA School, "Expert Interview with Lisa Beres on Making Homes Healthier," July 31, 2015. http://icaschool.com.

The goal of sustainable construction is to balance environmental, economic, and social concerns to meet present needs while not compromising future needs. As part of this goal, sustainable construction considers a project's effect on human health from any potential exposure to pollutants and chemicals.

According to the EPA, a growing body of research indicates that the air inside homes and buildings can contain a variety of harmful toxins and pollutants. With many people spending the majority of their time inside, the health risks from poor indoor air quality may be greater than the risks associated with outdoor air pollution. Prashant Kumar of the University of Surrey, who has researched indoor air quality, explains:

> When we think of the term "air pollution," we tend to think of car exhausts or factory fumes expelling gray smoke. However, there are actually various sources of pollution that have a negative effect on air quality, many of which are found inside our homes and offices. From cooking residue to paints, varnishes and fungal spores, the air we breathe indoors is often more polluted than that outside.[26]

Sources of Indoor Air Pollution

There are many sources of air pollution in homes and buildings. Smoke from oil, gas, kerosene, coal, wood, and tobacco products are common sources of indoor air pollution. Building materials and furnishings such as insulation, wet or damp carpet, cabinetry, or furniture made of certain pressed wood products can also release harmful chemicals and pollutants into the air. Other sources of indoor air pollution include the chemicals used in certain cleaning products, paints, and veneers; pesticides from pest management practices; and biological contaminants from dirty ventilation systems. All of these sources of indoor air pollution release gases or particles into the air that can be breathed in by building occupants.

The harmful effects of any single source depend on how much pollution it emits and how hazardous the pollutant is. Some sources, such as building materials, furnishings, and household products, emit pollutants continuously. Other sources, such as cigarettes, unvented stoves or furnaces, and cleaning solvents, emit pollutants only when used. When high concentrations of pollutants are released, they can remain in the air for a long time even after the activity has stopped. According to the EPA, levels of several organic gases emitted from paint, cleaning solvents, hobby supplies, and other products can average two to five times higher indoors than outdoors. In addition, during and immediately after certain activities, such as paint stripping, the levels of these gases may be one thousand times that of outdoor levels.

Improving Ventilation Systems

The quality of indoor air is directly related to the amount of ventilation in a building. Bringing in fresh, clean outside air can dilute emissions from indoor sources of pollutants, while circulating indoor air to the outside carries pollutants out of the building. If too little outside air enters a building, pollutants inside can accumulate, affecting the people who spend time inside.

Building ventilation systems can be mechanical or passive. Mechanical systems use fans to draw fresh outside air into a building. They provide consistent airflow and can control air speed, air

The chemicals used in some paints contribute to indoor air pollution. These chemicals release gases or particles into the air that occupants breathe.

quality, temperature, and humidity. However, if they are poorly designed or not operated and maintained properly, ventilation systems can add to indoor air pollution. When air supply and return vents are blocked, outdoor air does not reach the people inside the building. Improperly located outdoor air intake vents can draw in contaminated air if placed near automobile and truck exhaust, boiler emissions, dumpster fumes, or air vented from restrooms. If ventilation systems are not cleaned properly, biological contaminants can grow in cooling towers, humidifiers, dehumidifiers, air conditioners, and on the inside of air ducts. When the ventilation system circulates the air, it can spread the accumulated biological contaminants throughout the building.

When properly designed and integrated with filter systems, mechanical ventilation systems can improve indoor air quality.

SICK BUILDING SYNDROME

Sometimes people who live or work in a building experience health symptoms that do not fit the pattern of any specific illness. The symptoms are also difficult to trace back to a source. The building's occupants may complain of dry or burning mucous membranes in the nose, eyes, and throat. They may have a constant stuffy or runny nose and sneeze a lot. They may have a pervasive feeling of fatigue or lethargy or may experience headaches, dizziness, nausea, irritability, and forgetfulness. This phenomenon has been called sick building syndrome.

There is no consistent way sick building syndrome appears. Sometimes workers experience symptoms when they arrive at work, but these symptoms decrease when they leave for the night. Other times symptoms continue even outside of the building. In some cases many workers experience the same symptoms. In other cases only a few workers experience health problems. Some experts at the World Health Organization believe that sick building syndrome may be linked to poor indoor air quality. Potential solutions to sick building syndrome include removing the source of pollution, increasing ventilation, and cleaning a building's air ducts.

Mechanical filters and air cleaners can remove dust particles, mold spores, and pollen and animal dander from the air. Ultraviolet air purifiers use ultraviolet light to kill microorganisms like bacteria and viruses living in the building's ductwork and can also remove some gaseous pollutants like smoke and pesticides. One of the drawbacks of mechanical systems is that they consume energy to power the system.

Passive ventilation, also called natural ventilation, brings fresh outside air into a building without mechanical systems or fans. This type of system requires no maintenance or electrical power. Instead, passive ventilation systems depend on outside air movement and pressure differences to cool and ventilate a building. For example, the side of the building facing the wind has higher air pressure than the backside of the building. This difference in air pressure causes air to move through the building's vents and windows from the higher-pressure side to the lower-pressure side. Other systems work on the principle that hot air rises. This type of system captures warm, moist air in ducts and releases it through vents in the roof. Fresh air is then drawn in through vents in the walls or windows. However, because passive systems rely on outside air temperatures and weather patterns, they may not be as efficient at certain times of the day or months of the year.

Some hybrid ventilation systems combine passive ventilation techniques with efficient mechanical ventilation systems. For example, displacement ventilation uses mechanically supplied air at the floor level. The air is slightly cooler than would be desired. As the air moves horizontally across the floor, the heat from the interior building warms it and causes it to rise naturally. The rising air current moves the indoor air upward to exhaust vents in the ceiling, which take the air up and out of the room.

In 2015 researchers from Harvard University, SUNY Upstate Medical University, and Syracuse University studied the effect of well-ventilated offices on workers. They examined the impact of ventilation, chemicals, and carbon dioxide on a person's cognitive function. As buildings have become more energy efficient, they have also become more airtight, which increases the risk of poor indoor air quality. The researchers studied participants as they worked in a controlled office environment. For six days participants were exposed to various simulated building conditions while they performed their normal work. Researchers adjusted the concentrations of volatile organic compounds (VOCs), levels of carbon dioxide, and ventilation. At the end of each day, the researchers performed cognitive testing on the participants. They found that when the participants worked in well-ventilated offices with below-average levels of indoor pollutants and carbon dioxide, they performed significantly better in tests of cognitive functioning than when they worked in conditions with average levels of pollutants and carbon dioxide. The findings suggest that improved air quality could greatly increase the mental

> **WORDS IN CONTEXT**
>
> ---
>
> **VOCs**
> Volatile organic compounds that are emitted as gases from certain solids or liquids and may have adverse health effects.

performance of workers. "We spend 90% of our time indoors and 90% of the cost of a building are the occupants, yet indoor environmental quality and its impact on health and productivity are often an afterthought," says Joseph Allen, director of the Healthy Buildings Program at the Harvard Center for Health and the Global Environment and lead author of the study. "These results suggest that even modest improvements to indoor environmental quality may have a profound impact on the decision-making performance of workers."[27]

Reducing VOCs

VOCs are common air pollutants in buildings. They are emitted as gases from certain solids and liquids. VOCs include compounds like acetone, benzene, and formaldehyde. When inhaled, they can have short-term and long-term adverse health effects. Understanding VOC emissions and how to reduce them is an important part of sustainable construction. "Buildings, whether new or old, can have high levels of VOCs in them, sometimes so high that you can smell them,"[28] says Vadoud Niri, a researcher studying VOCs and indoor air quality.

A large number of products and materials used in buildings emit VOCs. Paints, varnishes, adhesives, and waxes all contain organic chemicals. Many cleaning, disinfecting, cosmetic, degreasing, and hobby products also contain organic chemicals, as do a variety of fuels. All of these products can release organic compounds during use and sometimes even when being stored. Many common building materials also add to VOC concentrations in the air, including carpets, wall panels, and furniture.

High concentrations of VOCs in indoor air can negatively affect a person's health. One common VOC, formaldehyde, is used in the manufacturing of building materials and many household products. It is also a by-product of combustion. According to the World Health Organization, prolonged exposure to levels of formaldehyde greater than one hundred parts per billion can cause sensory and respiratory irritation and nasal cancers.

Signs of VOC exposure include eye, nose, and throat discomfort; headache; allergic skin reactions; nausea; fatigue; and

Well-ventilated offices, with low levels of indoor pollutants and carbon dioxide, lead to better cognitive function by employees. To achieve energy efficiency, many buildings have become more airtight—which might actually result in poorer indoor air quality.

dizziness. Over time, repeated exposure to VOCs can damage the liver, kidneys, and central nervous system. Some VOCs can cause cancer in animals and are suspected to cause cancer in humans. "Inhaling large amounts of VOCs can lead some people to develop sick building syndrome, which reduces productivity and can even cause dizziness, asthma or allergies," Niri says. "We must do something about VOCs in indoor air."[29]

As buildings become more airtight to conserve energy, VOCs and other air pollutants build up inside. To create healthy indoor environments, scientists are working on ways to reduce VOC emissions. One strategy to reduce VOCs is to increase ventilation and cycle air in from outside. Another method is to reduce VOCs at the source; choosing products that have been tested for VOC emissions can help improve indoor air quality.

Hedgehog Particles

In 2015 a team of University of Michigan engineers reported that it had created a new process that would help manufacturers create more environmentally friendly paints. Most paints contain toxic VOCs like toluene, which is used to dissolve the paint's pigment. The engineers were looking for new ways to dissolve various types of particles without toxic chemicals. They created spiky microscopic particles, called hedgehog particles, by growing zinc oxide spikes on polystyrene microbeads. During this process, they discovered that the hedgehog particles could modify hydrophobic particles—molecules that typically do not dissolve in water—and allow them to disperse easily in water. The particles were also able to modify water-soluble particles, enabling them to dissolve in oil or oily chemicals. Nicholas Kotov, an engineering professor at the university, explains:

> We thought we'd made a mistake. We saw these particles that are supposed to hate water dispersing in it and we thought maybe the particles weren't hydrophobic, or maybe there was a chemical layer that was enabling them to disperse. But we double-checked everything and found that, in fact, these particles defy the conventional chemical wisdom that we all learned in high school.[30]

The tiny spikes made the particles repel each other more. The spikes also reduced the particles' surface area, which helped them diffuse more easily. The researchers say the process can be performed on almost any type of particle. In addition, they can vary the number and size of the spikes on the particle by adjusting the time the particle sits in various solutions to grow the spikes. They can also use materials other than zinc oxide to make the spikes.

According to the researchers, if pigments found in paints and coatings are made from spiky hedgehog particles, they could more easily be dissolved in nontoxic carriers such as water. As a result, manufacturers could use water instead of toxic chemicals like toluene, and fewer VOCs would be released from paints and coatings. "VOC solvents are toxic, they're flammable, they're expensive to handle and dispose of safely," Kotov says. "So if you can avoid using them, there's a significant cost savings in addition to environmental benefits."[31] He believes that hedgehog particles could provide a simple, versatile, and cost-effective way to manufacture low-VOC paints and coatings.

USING PLANTS TO IMPROVE INDOOR AIR QUALITY

Researchers are studying the effect that certain houseplants can have on VOCs. Bio-filtration or phytoremediation is the process of using plants to remove chemicals from indoor air. Plants can remove carbon dioxide, along with gases such as benzene, toluene, and other VOCs, by absorbing these compounds through their leaves and roots.

Vadoud Niri, a researcher at the State University of New York–Oswego, and his team built a sealed chamber that held specific concentrations of several VOCs. They measured VOC concentrations over several hours with and without different types of plants in the chamber. They noted which VOCs each plant took up, how quickly the plant removed the VOCs from the air, and how much of the VOCs were removed by the end of the test. They tested five common houseplants and eight common VOCs, finding that some plants were better at absorbing specific compounds. For example, while all five plants removed acetone from the air, the dracaena plant absorbed about 94 percent of the chemical from the air. "Based on our results, we can recommend what plants are good for certain types of VOCs and for specific locations," Niri says. "To illustrate, the bromeliad plant was very good at removing six out of eight studied VOCs—it was able to take up more than 80 percent of each of those compounds—over the twelve-hour sampling period. So it could be a good plant to have sitting around in the household or workplace."

Quoted in American Chemical Society, "Selecting the Right House Plant Could Improve Indoor Air Quality," ScienceDaily, August 24, 2016. ww.sciencedaily.com.

Better Filtration

In addition to VOC emissions, other substances such as mold spores, particulate matter, and other nonvolatile chemical emissions can affect indoor air quality. Air purifiers can help clean the air by passing it through a filter that removes particles. In homes these filters are usually part of the heating or cooling system. Typical filters are made from foam, cotton, fiberglass, or synthetic fibers. These filters remove small particles that are found in soot, smoke, and exhaust that can damage the lungs when inhaled. However, typical air filters are not able to capture chemical emissions such as carbon monoxide, formaldehyde, and other gaseous compounds.

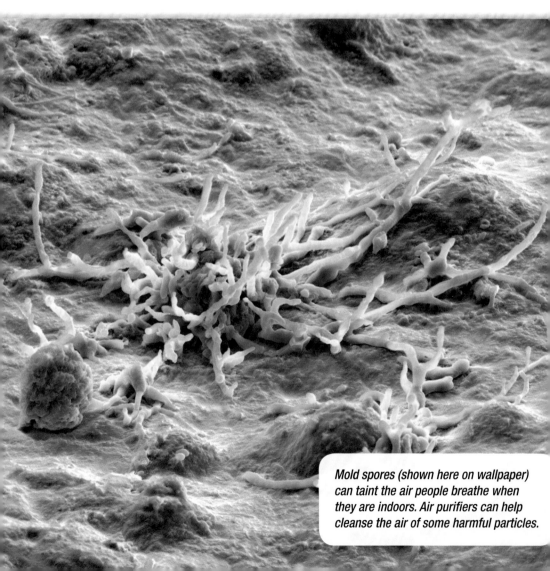

Mold spores (shown here on wallpaper) can taint the air people breathe when they are indoors. Air purifiers can help cleanse the air of some harmful particles.

Researchers at Washington State University have developed a soy-based air filter that can capture toxic chemicals that traditional filters miss, such as formaldehyde and carbon monoxide. Working with a team from the University of Science and Technology Beijing, the researchers developed the filter using natural, purified soy protein and bacterial cellulose, an organic compound produced by bacteria. The soy protein and cellulose are already used in several products, including adhesives, plastics, and wound dressings. Because soy contains a large number of functional chemical groups, it is very effective at capturing chemical pollution. Each chemical group can attract and capture passing pollution at the molecular level. "We can take advantage from those chemical groups to grab the [toxins] in the air,"[32] says Weihong Zhong, a professor in the Washington State University School of Mechanical and Materials Engineering. As a result, the soy filter is able to remove nearly all of the small particles in the air as well as chemical pollutants. In addition, the soy filter is cost effective and biodegradable, as soybeans are one of the most abundant plants in the world. "Air pollution is a very serious health issue," says Zhong. "If we can improve indoor air quality, it would help a lot of people."[33]

WORDS IN CONTEXT

bio-filtration
The process of using plants to remove chemicals from indoor air.

CHAPTER FIVE

Using Water Efficiently

Clean water is a critical natural resource and is vital to the survival of every living thing on earth. Although it may appear that the earth has an endless and abundant supply of water, only 1 percent of Earth's water is actually available for human use. The remaining water is salt water in the oceans, is frozen freshwater in polar ice caps, or is located in places that are too difficult to reach.

Around the world, human population growth and pollution are rapidly depleting the planet's sources of clean water. In the United States alone, the average family uses more than 300 gallons (1,136 L) of water per day at home, according to the EPA. About 70 percent of this use occurs indoors. Although the water cycle continuously returns water to earth, it does not always return it to the same place, in the same quantity, or with the same quality. According to the World Wide Fund for Nature, at the current consumption rate, two-thirds of the world's population may face water shortages by 2025. Ecosystems around the world will suffer.

Managing water supplies has become an increasing challenge in the United States and in communities around the world. Many communities with large population growth and high water usage can expect that competition for water resources will increase. When reservoir water levels and water tables drop, water supplies, human health, and ecosystems are at risk. For example, lower water levels can lead to higher concentrations of water pollutants. More efficient use of water will enable water supplies to remain at safe levels. Less water being used means more water in the lakes, streams, and rivers that ecosystems need for life. Using water more efficiently protects supplies, health, and the environment.

With these concerns in mind, sustainable construction can play an important role in smart water use. Buildings use a significant amount of water. However, there are sustainable strategies that can be deployed to reduce the amount of water used, including designing efficient water systems, detecting leaks, installing water-conservation technologies, and implementing water reuse and recycling programs.

Metering and Detecting Leaks

It is difficult to manage something that is not measured. Tracking a building's total water use, in particular its specific uses, is a critical step in making sustainable construction choices and improving a facility's water efficiency. Using meters to accurately measure water use allows facility managers and homeowners to identify areas where water usage can be reduced. They can also use measurements from meters to record progress once water-efficient technologies and procedures have been put in place. Other types of meters can help identify when and where a leak occurs and alert occupants when equipment malfunctions.

Water meters and submeters can be part of a building's centralized management system, which makes it simple to track water usage and develop a water-management plan. These meters and systems can report water use at specific intervals, such as hourly, daily, monthly, and annually. Meters and submeters can also quickly alert building managers and homeowners to a leak. On average, undetected leaks can account for more than 6 percent of a facility's total water use, according to the EPA. For example, a toilet leaking 0.5 gallons (1.9 L) per minute loses 21,600 gallons (81,765 L) of water per month. An unattended water hose that releases 10 gallons (38 L) per minute loses 5,400 gallons (20,441 L) per day. And a broken water distribution line can leak 8,100 gallons (30,662 L) of water in a single night. Therefore, monitoring and measuring systems that alert users to leaks so that they can be quickly repaired can greatly minimize water waste.

Water-Efficient Landscapes

Buildings use a significant amount of water, both inside and outside. Outside, a building's landscaping requires a lot of water, sometimes as much as 20 percent or more of a facility's water consumption, according to the National Institute of Building Sciences. Several strategies can reduce the amount of water needed and create a water-efficient landscape. First, selecting native plants that are tolerant to a specific climate can reduce the need for extra watering. Many native plants can survive on rainwater alone once they have matured. Because turf grasses typically need a lot of water, reducing the amount of turf grasses reduces irrigation needs and conserves water.

Any remaining landscape areas that need irrigation can use water-efficient irrigation systems. These systems use low-flow sprinkler heads and provide only enough water to keep the landscape healthy. Techniques such as drip irrigation and micro sprayers direct small amounts of water to specific plant areas, which helps eliminate runoff. Drip irrigation allows water to drip slowly to the roots of plants through a network of valves, pipes, and tubes. Micro sprayers operate under low pressure to deliver water through micro tubing to a series of nozzles attached to risers. Irrigation controllers allow for seasonal adjustment and timed irrigation schedules that help minimize water use while still keeping plants healthy. For example, irrigation controllers allow landscapers to reduce irrigation during heavy rain. In addition, water-efficient landscapes tend to have mulch and compost around plants to conserve moisture in the soil and reduce surface water

Drip irrigation (pictured) and micro sprayers help eliminate runoff by directing small amounts of water to the soil around plant roots. Getting rid of spray from overhead sprinklers also leads to healthier plants.

evaporation. Sites can also be designed to direct rainwater runoff to other planting areas in order to take advantage of rainwater.

Water-Efficient Buildings

Inside buildings, significant water savings can occur with improvements in equipment and operational practices. Every type of building has different water use patterns depending on its function, from residential homes and schools to office buildings and restaurants. Regardless of a building's function, several water-efficiency techniques can be implemented across a wide variety of facilities with varying water needs. Implementing water-efficiency strategies can help a building reduce operational costs as well as achieve sustainability goals. In addition to saving water, the building will also save energy because of a reduced need for water heating.

Bathroom plumbing fixtures are responsible for a significant portion of indoor water use. According to the National Institute of Building Sciences, toilet and urinal flushing account for nearly one-

STORM WATER MANAGEMENT

Strategies that collect rainwater can also reduce storm water runoff. Storm water runoff can have several damaging effects on the environment. It can wash away unprotected topsoil, which can lead to erosion and soil displacement. It can carry soil into undesirable areas, such as streams or storm drains. There the soil can damage the water quality of rivers, streams, lakes, and oceans and damage wildlife habitats. It can also clog storm drains, which can cause flooding. And if it picks up and carries toxic pollutants, water runoff can contaminate the areas it reaches.

Sustainable construction attempts to minimize the amount of storm water runoff that leaves a site. It uses site and landscape features such as rain gardens, planter boxes, and permeable pavements to trap the water and collect it for reuse or allow it to soak into the ground. In general, impervious materials such as asphalt, concrete, and traditional roofs do not allow water to soak into the ground. Therefore, a sustainable design uses less of these materials and features.

third of a building's total water consumption. This area is one of the simplest in which to implement water-efficient technologies. Low-flow toilets and urinals use less water while still maintaining their function. Dual-flush toilets allow users to choose a smaller flush with less water for liquid waste or a larger flush for solid waste. Some buildings have installed waterless urinals. These fixtures are made with a urine-repellent surface, have no flush handles, and require virtually no water. A chemical in the bowl pushes the liquid waste into the drain without using water. With proper maintenance, the waterless urinal performs as well as traditional urinals.

Composting toilets are another option for sustainable building. This type of toilet does not require the use of water or electricity. Instead, it relies on the natural processes of decomposition and evaporation to recycle human waste. Liquid waste evaporates and is carried back to the atmosphere through a vent system. Solid waste decomposes into natural fertilizing soil. An effective decomposition process requires a proper balance between oxygen, moisture, heat, and organic material in the composting chamber. This balance creates a rich environment for the aerobic bacteria that decompose the waste and transform it into fertilizing soil. When the waste is properly composted, any pathogens or viruses it contains are destroyed by bacteria. The resulting nutrient-rich fertilizer can be used on plants or at the base of trees, reducing the need for commercial fertilizers.

In Seattle's six-story Bullitt Center building, which opened in 2013, composting toilets work to sustainably transform human waste into mulch that will eventually be commingled with other compost from the area. Every flush mixes from 1 tablespoon to 1 cup (14.8 mL to 237 mL) of water with biodegradable soap to form foam that helps the waste make its way through the system into blue composting bins. A hand crank turns the material, like a home backyard composting system. The waste is eventually transformed into a natural fertilizer.

Water Harvest, Reuse, and Recycling

Many buildings have water use needs that can be met with non-potable water. Nonpotable water is water that has not been examined, treated, or approved as being safe for consumption. While it cannot be used for drinking or cooking, nonpotable water may still be used for many other purposes, such as laundry or toilet flushing. Using nonpotable water reduces potable water use and also saves on sewage costs. Often, the building's architects need to consider water harvest, reuse, and recycling needs early in the design process in order to be successful. Several strategies can be employed, including on-site water reuse or recycling, water catchment systems, and reuse of gray water.

> **WORDS IN CONTEXT**
>
> **nonpotable**
> Describes water that is not safe for human consumption.

On-site water reuse or recycling reuses water from the same purpose at the same location. One example of on-site water reuse is taking rinse water filtered from washing machines and reusing it in the next laundry wash cycle. This type of reuse usually requires minimal treatment or filtration of the water. Another example occurs at industrial sites, where companies reuse water used in cooling processes.

Water catchment systems capture rainwater. Rainwater run-off is generated when natural precipitation such as rain or snow falls on the site. Water catchment systems capture the rainwater through different site features such as cisterns and rain barrels and funnel it through roof drains and filters. The captured rainwater can be stored in cisterns, basins, or tanks and used for landscape irrigation. Excess water can be stored and used for irrigation during dry months. Rainwater can also be used inside a building to flush toilets and for other nonpotable water needs. In some cases collected rainwater can be filtered so that it is suitable for drinking.

As rooftop water catchment systems become more popular, researchers in Texas are studying the effect of roofing materials on harvested rainwater. "Rainwater harvesting is becoming fairly widespread, at least in Central Texas. There's interest born out of necessity because people are simply running out of water in rural areas or they're interested in conserving water supplies and it's good for the environment,"[34] says Sanjeev Kalaswad, the Texas Water Development Board's rainwater harvesting coordinator.

To understand what types of roof surfaces are best for rainwater collection, a team of professors and engineering students at the University of Texas–Austin Cockrell School of Engineering conducted an in-depth study. Over a year, they examined water collected from five roofing materials: asphalt fiberglass shingle; Galvalume, a type of metal roof; concrete tile; cool, a type of roof that reflects sunlight; and vegetation and growing medium (used in green roofs). The researchers found that metal, concrete tile, and cool roofs produced the highest quality of harvested rainwater for indoor use. They also found that rainwater collected from asphalt fiberglass shingle roofs and popular green roofing materials had high levels of dissolved organic carbon (DOC). While other potential pollutants and issues, such as aluminum or turbidity,

> ### WORDS IN CONTEXT
>
> **gray water**
> Water captured from showers, bathtubs, sinks, and washing machines; does not include wastewater from toilets.

were significantly lower on green roofs, the high levels of DOC were significant if the roofs were to be used for potable rainwater collection. Although water with DOC is not itself dangerous, mixing it with chlorine, a substance commonly used to disinfect water, produces by-products that could cause cancer and have other adverse health effects. "Someone who already has a rainwater system is probably not going to change their roofing material based on this study, but this information is useful for anyone who's trying to make an informed decision about what material to use,"[35] says engineering assistant professor Mary Jo Kirisits. While some roofing materials performed better, Kirisits cautioned that rainwater harvested from any of the roofs would still need to be treated to meet the EPA's drinking water standards.

A system for capturing and storing rainwater (pictured) can be used for irrigation and also for toilet flushing. Rainwater catchment systems are gaining in popularity.

Gray Water Reuse

Gray water is water captured from showers, bathtubs, sinks, and washing machines. It does not include water used in diaper washing or food processing. Gray water may contain traces of dirt, food, grease, hair, and certain household cleaning products. Gray water must be processed and filtered before reuse to meet federal and state health standards. To capture gray water, plumbing systems must be set up to funnel water from toilets, the kitchen sink, and the dishwasher to one tank, while water from bathroom sinks, showers, bathtubs, and washing machines funnels to a

SAVING WATER IN SHOWERS AND SINKS

Low-flow showerheads and faucets can be installed to save significant amounts of water and the energy used to heat water. New showerheads have a narrower spray area and a greater mix of air and water. As a result, less water is used, but the user does not feel a difference in quality or comfort. New models of low-flow showerheads feature atomizers to deliver water in small droplets over larger surface areas, pulsators that vary spray patterns, and aerators that mix water droplets with air to increase water coverage.

Low-flow faucets also use aeration technology and sensors to reduce water use. Newer low-flow faucet technologies include metered valves that deliver a certain amount of water and then automatically shut off, self-closing faucets that shut off a few seconds after the faucet is turned on, and ultrasonic and infrared sensors that automatically turn on the faucet when a user's hands are beneath it and turn it off when the user removes his or her hands.

In 2014 Kennesaw State University in Kennesaw, Georgia, replaced thirty-six hundred showerheads in dormitories and athletic facilities on campus with low-flow alternatives. In the six months after the showerhead switch, the university saved 666,000 gallons (2.5 million L) of water, about 28 percent of the water used in the dorms. The students using the low-flow showerheads did not report any loss of comfort or function. "We've only gotten positive feedback," says Kathy Nguyen, a senior project manager for Cobb County Water System. "They've been really happy with them."

Quoted in US Environmental Protection Agency, "Cobb County Showers KSU with Campus-Wide Savings," October 2015. www3.epa.gov.

How a Basic Gray Water System Works

Gray water systems divert household waste water for various uses, including plant irrigation. A basic gray water system pipes water from washing machines, sinks, and showers into a septic tank (or surge tank). The tank holds the initial surge of waste water only until it flows into the filter. Sand filters, which are common, often include shallow layers of stone, gravel, and sand. The filter prevents hair, lint, food particles, and other solid materials from reaching plants. The filtered water then passes through a pump, which sends the water to designated areas for watering plants and trees.

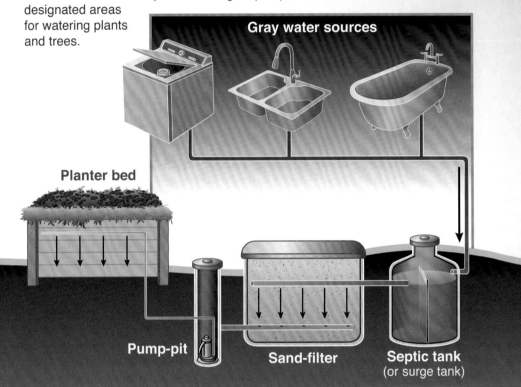

Gray water sources

Planter bed

Pump-pit

Sand-filter

Septic tank
(or surge tank)

Source: Lafayette College, "The Governance of Technology: Grey Water and Recycled Water System." http://sites.lafayette.edu.

separate tank. The water from the second tank is then sent to a treatment system. Commercial gray water treatment systems use natural treatment such as live plants, microorganisms, and bacteria to clean the water. Some use mechanical filtration. Once the water has been filtered and processed, it can be reused for landscape irrigation and toilet flushing.

Because some people have concerns that using gray water can increase the risk of gastrointestinal illness or other water-borne diseases, scientists at the Zuckerberg Institute for Water Research at Ben-Gurion University of the Negev in Israel conducted a study to examine the health effects of gray water used by the study's participants. In the study, gray water included any wastewater generated in a house or office building except wastewater from toilets. According to the researchers, "There is a growing interest in greywater reuse from sinks, bathtubs and laundry machines, particularly in water-scarce regions. New greywater systems, including one developed at the Zuckerberg Institute, now make reuse economically feasible on both a national and household scale, provided it is handled responsibly to eliminate potential environmental and health risks."[36]

Researchers divided study participants into two groups: gray water users and non–gray water users. Participants completed a weekly health questionnaire for a year. They also completed a lifestyle questionnaire to determine their exposure level to gray water or potable water used to water gardens and landscapes. The researchers found that treated gray water was safe for irrigation and did not pose an increased health risk for gastrointestinal illness or water-related diseases. "In fact, the rate of illnesses was found to be lower with the treated greywater than from the control group at times, suggesting that the main exposure to gastrointestinal disease-causing bacteria is not likely from exposure to pathogens in greywater,"[37] explains Amit Gross, a professor at the Zuckerberg Institute. As a follow-up to this initial study, Gross recommends that scientists further research the possible connection between gastrointestinal illnesses and exposure to gray water with a larger population.

The Future of Science in Sustainable Construction

From developing sustainable materials to finding ways to improve air quality, science and technology will be at the forefront of new developments in sustainable construction. With research and new technologies, communities will be able to create buildings and structures that are environmentally friendly, socially responsible, and economically beneficial, meeting the needs of the present while protecting those of the future.

SOURCE NOTES

Introduction: Building a Sustainable World

1. Quoted in National Association for Environmental Management, "What Is Sustainability?," 2017. www.naem.org.
2. Ban Ki-moon, "The Road to Dignity by 2030: Ending Poverty, Transforming All Lives and Protecting the Planet," United Nations, December 2014. www.un.org.
3. Quoted in PRNewswire, "New Report Highlights Latest Global Green Building Trends and Projections," November 15, 2015. www.prnewswire.com.
4. Ban Ki-moon, "The Road to Dignity by 2030."

Chapter One: History of Sustainable Construction

5. Quoted in David Hill, "Bullitt Center: Benchmarking the Benchmark," *Architect Magazine*, December 1, 2016. http://bullitt center.architectmagazine.com.
6. Denis Hayes, "Better, Faster, More: Toward Sustainable Cities," Bullitt Center. www.bullittcenter.org.

Chapter Two: Using Energy Efficiently

7. Quoted in Oak Ridge National Laboratory, "Energy Use in Buildings: Innovative, Lower Cost Sensors and Controls Yield Better Energy Efficiency," ScienceDaily, February 27, 2015. www.sciencedaily.com.
8. Quoted in Oak Ridge National Laboratory, "Energy Use in Buildings."
9. Quoted in Frances White, "Electricity Use Slashed with Efficiency Controls for Heating, Cooling," Pacific Northwest National Laboratory, May 23, 2014. www.pnnl.gov.
10. Quoted in White, "Electricity Use Slashed with Efficiency Controls for Heating, Cooling."
11. Quoted in Universiti Putra Malaysia, "New Nano Tech to Cool Down Buildings," ScienceDaily, July 27, 2016. www.science daily.com.
12. Quoted in American Chemical Society, "A Brighter Design Emerges for Low-Cost, 'Greener' LED Light Bulbs," ScienceDaily, October 15, 2014. www.sciencedaily.com.

13. Quoted in University of Toronto Faculty of Applied Science & Engineering, "Bio-inspired Design May Lead to More Energy Efficient Windows," ScienceDaily, August 2, 2013. www.sciencedaily.com.
14. Quoted in University of Toronto Faculty of Applied Science & Engineering, "Bio-inspired Design May Lead to More Energy Efficient Windows."
15. Quoted in General Services Administration, "Plug Load Control," September 2012. www.gsa.gov.
16. Quoted in Imperial College London, "Tiny 'LEGO Brick'–Style Studs Make Solar Panels a Quarter More Efficient," ScienceDaily, October 18, 2013. www.sciencedaily.com.
17. Quoted in Sandia National Laboratories, "Battling Corrosion to Keep Solar Panels Humming," ScienceDaily, February 2, 2017. www.sciencedaily.com.
18. Quoted in Sandia National Laboratories, "Battling Corrosion to Keep Solar Panels Humming."

Chapter Three: Building with Sustainable Materials
19. Quoted in DVIRC, "Report Shows Value of Building Reuse, Retrofitting," January 26, 2012. www.dvirc.org.
20. Quoted in Rutgers University, "Recycled Plastic Lumber Invented," ScienceDaily, July 7, 2016. www.sciencedaily.com.
21. Quoted in Rutgers University, "Recycled Plastic Lumber Invented."
22. Quoted in Universiti Putra Malaysia, "Turning Sewage Sludge into Concrete," ScienceDaily, August 28, 2015. www.sciencedaily.com.
23. Quoted in University of Notre Dame, "Why Not Recycled Concrete?," ScienceDaily, February 8, 2016. www.sciencedaily.com.
24. Quoted in University of Notre Dame, "Why Not Recycled Concrete?"
25. Quoted in Armstrong Flooring, "Case Study: Bio Flooring," 2017. www.armstrongflooring.com.

Chapter Four: Improving Indoor Air Quality
26. Quoted in Robert Ferris, "Indoor Air Can Be Deadlier than Outdoor Air, Research Shows," CNBC, April 22, 2016. www.cnbc.com.

27. Quoted in Harvard T.H. Chan School of Public Health, "Green Office Environments Linked with Higher Cognitive Function Scores," ScienceDaily, October 26, 2015. www.sciencedaily .com.
28. Quoted in American Chemical Society, "Selecting the Right House Plant Could Improve Indoor Air Quality," ScienceDaily, August 24, 2016. www.sciencedaily.com.
29. Quoted in American Chemical Society, "Selecting the Right House Plant Could Improve Indoor Air Quality."
30. Quoted in University of Michigan, "Spiky 'Hedgehog Particles' for Safer Paints, Fewer VOC Emissions," ScienceDaily, January 28, 2015. www.sciencedaily.com.
31. Quoted in University of Michigan, "Spiky 'Hedgehog Particles' for Safer Paints, Fewer VOC Emissions."
32. Quoted in Washington State University, "Environmentally-Friendly Soy Air Filter Developed: Soy-Based Filter Can Capture Toxic Chemicals That Other Filters Can't," ScienceDaily, January 13, 2017. www.sciencedaily.com.
33. Quoted in Washington State University, "Environmentally-Friendly Soy Air Filter Developed."

Chapter Five: Using Water Efficiently

34. Quoted in University of Texas at Austin Cockrell School of Engineering, "Rainwater Harvesting Study," March 3, 2011. www.engr.utexas.edu.
35. Quoted in University of Texas at Austin Cockrell School of Engineering, "Rainwater Harvesting Study."
36. Quoted in American Associates, Ben-Gurion University of the Negev, "Greywater Reuse for Irrigation Is Safe, Study Shows," ScienceDaily, December 16, 2015. www.sciencedaily.com.
37. Quoted in American Associates, Ben-Gurion University of the Negev, "Greywater Reuse for Irrigation Is Safe, Study Shows."

FIND OUT MORE

Books

Avi Friedman, *Sustainable: Houses with Small Footprints*. New York: Rizzoli, 2015.

Charles J. Kibert, *Sustainable Construction: Green Building Design and Delivery*. 4th ed. Hoboken, NJ: Wiley, 2016.

Ellen Labrecque, *Green General Contractor*. Ann Arbor, MI: Cherry Lake, 2017.

Norbert Lechner, *Heating, Cooling, Lighting: Sustainable Design Methods for Architects*. Hoboken, NJ: Wiley, 2015.

William Maclay, *The New Net Zero: Leading-Edge Design and Construction of Homes and Buildings for a Renewable Energy Future*. White River Junction, VT: Chelsea Green, 2014.

Chris Magwood, *Making Better Buildings: A Comparative Guide to Sustainable Construction for Homeowners and Contractors*. Gabriola Island, BC: New Society, 2014.

Robert Snedden, *Environmental Engineering and the Science of Sustainability*. St. Catharines, ON: Crabtree, 2014.

Saranne Taylor, Moreno Chiacchiera, and Michelle Todd, *Green Homes*. St. Catharines, ON: Crabtree, 2015.

Websites

Green Building Alliance (www.go-gba.org). The Green Building Alliance website has information about green building, LEED certification, and green building events and initiatives. It also has links to blog posts, the organization's magazine, and past newsletters.

Sustainability, US Environmental Protection Agency (www .epa.gov). This website has an entire section devoted to sustainability to help readers learn what sustainability is and why they should care about it. It also has a Greener Living subsection that has information about choices that everyday people can make in their lives to live more sustainably.

US Green Building Council (www.usgbc.org). This website has information about LEED certification, current articles about sustainable construction initiatives, and a calendar of sustainable construction events across the country. It also has a section that highlights sustainable building projects around the world.

Internet Sources

Adam Groff, "The Construction Industry Looks to Renewable Energy and Sustainability," Renewable Energy, October 1, 2015. www.energydigital.com/renewableenergy/3951/The-construction-industry-looks-to-renewable-energy-and-sustainability.

Lafarge Holcim Foundation, "Understanding Sustainable Construction," 2015. www.lafargeholcim-foundation.org/AboutPages /what-is-sustainable-construction.

Marble Institute, "Green Building." www.marble-institute.com/de fault/assets/File/consumers/historystoneingreenbuilding.pdf.

WBDG Sustainable Committee, "Sustainable," Whole Building Design Guide, 2017. www.wbdg.org/design-objectives/sustain able.

INDEX

PICTURE CREDITS

ABOUT THE AUTHOR

Carla Mooney is the author of many books for young adults and children. She lives in Pittsburgh, Pennsylvania, with her husband and three children.